DISCERNING GOD'S WILL
GROUP BIBLE STUDY

WRITTEN BY Russ Siders

Discerning God's Will: Group Bible Study
Written by Russ Siders
© 2020 Warner Press Inc.

Requests for information should be sent to:
Warner Press Inc.
P.O. Box 2499
Anderson, IN 46018
www.warnerpress.org

Unless otherwise noted, all Scripture references are from the Holy Bible, New International Version®, NIV® Copyright © 1973, 1978, 1984, 2011 by Biblica, Inc.® All rights reserved worldwide.

Kevin Stiffler • Editor
S. Katie Miller • Layout & Design

CONTENTS

The Warner Press *Relevance* Group Bible Studies provide intriguing examinations of topics using the whole of the Scriptures. The guides incorporate various stories and activities to introduce and apply the subject matter, with a Bible study component at the heart of each session. Our goal is to show life-long believers and those new to the faith how to know the Lord intimately while encouraging them to step out and join him in his work with miraculous results.

These flexible studies are ideal for any setting. We know that time is a valuable commodity in today's society, and that's why each book consists of five or six short lessons intended to meet the group's scheduling needs.

L1

Paying Attention

Numbers 22:1–35; Galatians 3:13

Main Point

In order to discern God's will, it is more important for us to pay attention to what God is doing right now than to focus on what we are going to do down the road.

Background

After forty years in the wilderness, God's people Israel were nearing their goal of entering the Promised Land. Along the way, they defeated two kings who stood against them. As the Israelites neared the country of Moab, King Balak was afraid that his army would be defeated next. He sent for a holy man named Balaam and asked him to come put a curse on the Israelites in order to keep them from overrunning his land. In Numbers 24:3, Balaam described himself as a prophet "whose eye sees clearly." In today's story, however, we will discover that Balaam's vision was not quite as good as advertised.

Distractions

Distraction is a major issue in our society today. One survey suggests that people may spend nearly half of their waking hours daydreaming about something other than what they are doing at the moment. Even as our attention spans dwindle, many of us carry with us a device that actually trains us to be distracted: the smart phone! Wherever we go, technology seems to be there—to help us navigate traffic, to remind us of appointments, even to recommend where to eat. With this kind of information at our fingertips, it can be tempting to think of God as a kind of voice-activated guide, ready at a moment's notice to serve our needs. The Bible, however, gives us a much different understanding of God's place, and ours, in the grand scheme of things. Discerning God's will is not about getting God to pay attention to us; rather, it's about learning to pay attention to God.

What routine activities can cause you to become easily distracted? Why?

What are some signs of spiritual distraction that you have experienced in your relationship with God?

I. **Read** Numbers 22:1–14.

Describe the fear factors that were behind King Balak's decision to send for Balaam. What was the king afraid of and why? What result did King Balak hope to get from cursing the people of Israel?

Balak noted that whomever Balaam blessed would be blessed and whomever he cursed would be cursed. What does Genesis 12:3 say about the people of Israel? What problem might this have presented for Balaam?

What determined Balaam's initial response to the representatives of King Balak?

II. Read Numbers 22:15–20.

How did King Balak respond to Balaam's refusal to curse Israel? Why?

____

____

____

What is the one caveat God gave when he allowed Balaam to go with Balak's men? What is significant about this?

____

____

____

III. Read Numbers 22:21–30.

What did the donkey see on the road? What did Balaam see? What was ironic about their different perspectives? Describe a situation when your own perspective was skewed but later became more accurate. What caused the change?

____

____

____

____

Verse 27 says that Balaam was angry with his donkey. Verse 22 says that God was very angry with Balaam. How might these two details be related to each other?

Who emerged as the one "whose eye sees clearly" in this story? Who emerged as the stubborn "donkey"? What was significant about this?

IV. Read Numbers 22:31–35.

How was Balaam finally able to recognize what was going on?

Verse 32 is difficult for translators to render clearly in English. It might be helpful to compare several different Bible versions in order to get a better sense of what the text is saying here. In your opinion, what was the real problem that God identified in verse 32? Explain.

____

____

____

____

____

What did God want from Balaam, according to verse 35?

____

____

____

The story of Balaam and his donkey is filled with irony. Through an odd reversal of roles between these two characters, God was revealing something about spiritual discernment, including the importance of humility and the value of paying attention to the present moment. Often when we talk of discerning the will of God, we are looking so far down the road of our lives that we fail to notice what is right in front of us. We can become so distracted trying to figure out God's will for tomorrow that we fail to pay attention to what God wants from us today. How can a preoccupation with the future cause our way to become reckless?

V. Read Galatians 3:13.

How is Jesus different from Balaam? How does Jesus set us free from the curse of sin?

As we anticipate and participate in each day's activities, we have the opportunity to encounter Jesus and his blessings in our lives. How might we discover God's will as we bless the people in front of us?

The Power of Blessing

There is real power in blessing others. What seems to be a small gesture can become an opportunity for the Lord to show himself—to others and to us. One day as Dean came out of a local department store, he found himself slowed down by an elderly man pushing a shopping cart. Although Dean was in a hurry to get to his car, he patiently stayed behind the man, who continued in the same direction. As the man stopped to park the shopping cart, Dean noticed that he was wearing a cap identifying him as a war veteran. "Thank you for your service to our country," Dean said to him.

A gentle smile came to the man's face. "I'm just glad I made it back," he said. As Dean got into his car, he realized that what had seemed like an inconvenience was really a divine appointment. He paused to thank God for this man's sacrifice, and for the sacrifice of Jesus on the cross.

Divine appointments are moments when God makes his presence evident in our ordinary lives. What divine appointments can you recognize from this past week? What are some signs of God's presence you have observed?

Connecting with Creation

In the course of a typical day, we spend much of our time staring at all kinds of screens, including the television, computers, phones, and other devices. The result is that, like Balaam, we can become unaware of what God is doing right in front of us. One antidote to this tendency is to take a few minutes each day to contemplate some aspect of God's creation. Staring at a sunset, watching the breeze rustle the trees, or gazing at a flower—these can all be ways of linking the creation with the Creator. Another way is by simply watching people and remembering that each person we meet is made in the image of God.

In Thornton Wilder's play *Our Town*, one of the characters, Emily, asks, "Do any human beings realize life while they live it—every, every minute?" Paying attention to God's ordinary gifts can help us to give thanks for the extraordinary gift of God's presence in every single moment of life.

What is your favorite way of connecting with God's creation? How can you carve out some time in your daily schedule to pause, to ponder, and to pray?

Finding the Clues

As we go to work, to the store, or even to church, the roads we travel are so familiar to us that we often miss the signposts indicating where God is needed, or where God is at work. As you drive around your community—whether you live in a major city, a small town, or some other setting—be on the lookout for clues. Who is walking the streets? What kinds of cars do you see in traffic? In what condition are the businesses? How many Christian churches do you notice? What kinds of community agencies advertise their services? What are the schools like? Discerning God's will often begins by simply looking at our surroundings, with both physical and spiritual eyes.

Think about your own church. How would you describe the people who make up your congregation? Why?

What gifts and abilities do the people in your church possess? How might God use the talents of your church family to impact an apparent need in your community?

What are some ways you can work with other Christians in your area to be a blessing to your neighbors and a witness for Jesus Christ?

____

____

____

____

Closing Prayer

Heavenly Father, we confess that too often we fall into the trap of Balaam. We get so distracted that we fail to pay attention to your continual presence. Help us to discern your will by opening our eyes to what is in front of us. Thank you for sending Jesus to remove the curse of sin so that we can be a blessing to others in our world who need the love of God. Amen. ■

L2

Beware of Mission Drift

1 Samuel 15:1–23; Luke 9:51–56

Main Point

As we seek to discern God's will, we need to beware of mission drift, the tendency to confuse following our own goals with obeying God's plan.

Background

After the people of Israel settled in the Promised Land, they slowly veered away from their original mission of showing God's light to the nations around them. Idolatry was a constant temptation. Eventually, however, Israel fell into another trap. They wanted a king, so that they could be like everyone else. In spite of this rejection of his divine rule, God allowed the people to have a king and he even chose a man for the job: Saul. While Saul was tall, head and shoulders above the rest, he ultimately fell short of God's expectations. The culprit was a familiar one—mission drift.

Staying On Track

As the first astronauts traveled to the moon, they had a simple computer guidance system to help them home in on their goal. In addition to this technology, however, they needed to check their position every day by looking out the window at the stars. If they failed to take these measurements and make periodic course corrections, their spaceship would slowly but surely wander off target. Missing the moon would send the entire crew into deep space with no hope of return.

God provides us with wisdom from the Bible to orient us to his purpose for our lives. The Scriptures are an indispensable tool to guide us, but in order to benefit fully from this great gift, we need to monitor our position on a regular basis. Second Corinthians 13:5 says, "Examine yourselves to see whether you are in the faith; test yourselves." Spiritual course corrections are necessary to keep us from floating past God's will as shown in his Word.

Describe a recent project, such as a road trip or home improvement task, that ended up taking you to a much different place from where you intended. What factors caused you to get off track?

I. Read 1 Samuel 15:1–6.

Who was the messenger that came to Saul? Who was the author of the message he brought?

According to verse 2, what had the Amalekites done to Israel? What is your response to the order God gave to annihilate the Amalekites? How does Deuteronomy 25:17–19 change your understanding of who the Amalekites were? What did God ask Israel to do in verse 19? How did this affect the urgency of what God asked of Saul in 1 Samuel 15:3?

II. Read 1 Samuel 15:7–12.

Where did the first evidence crop up that Saul had drifted away from God's plan? What was this "drift"? From what you know so far, what might have been Saul's reasoning?

Where did Saul's rabbit trail end up, according to verse 12? What was the problem with this?

III. **Read** 1 Samuel 15:13–23.

What explanation did Saul give for his behavior? How did Samuel respond to Saul's excuse? Why?

Look at verses 20 and 21. How did Saul try to justify his actions? Do you think he had a solid case? Why or why not?

Saul believed that he was engaging in a kind of "creative obedience." What was Samuel's perspective in verses 22 and 23?

Looking back at Genesis 3:1–6, how did the serpent convince the woman that eating the forbidden fruit was good? At what point did the man and the woman drift from God's original mission for them?

Through the prophet Samuel, God gave King Saul very clear instructions regarding the battle plan against the Amalekites. In spite of a clear mission objective, Saul somehow convinced himself that he could improve on God's plan and that he could take a different route to obeying God's word. What Saul might have called creative obedience was really disobedience and rebellion against the Lord. Because of this, Saul forfeited his place as the legitimate king of Israel. His hard-hearted refusal to line up with God's will would ultimately lead him to his doom. When have you used creative reasoning to justify deviating from the expectations of a parent, a teacher, a supervisor, or someone else in authority over you? How did this person respond? What was the ultimate outcome of the situation?

IV. Read Luke 9:51–56.

What was Jesus' mission here? What did the disciples want Jesus to do? How did Jesus' response compare to Saul's in 1 Samuel 15?

How did Jesus' obedience to God set him apart as the King who is "head and shoulders" above the rest?

Missing the Mark

What is the target, the goal each day we live as followers of Jesus? What is the good that God wants us to pursue? Micah 6:8 says that it is "to act justly and to love mercy and to walk humbly with your God." Justice and mercy have to do with loving our neighbors by treating them with complete fairness and kindness. Walking humbly with God has to do with loving the Lord with all our heart and soul and mind and strength, honoring him above all.

Take a few minutes to think over your day so far. Where have you been able to live on target? Where might you have missed the mark of God's will? Remember, God understands the intent of our hearts. And confession and repentance are good things—they lead to forgiveness and a new start. How can you seek God's help for those instances of mission drift that come to mind?

What are some spiritual disciplines that Christians can practice in order to stay on target as Jesus followers?

What spiritual disciplines are part of your relationship with the Lord? How do they help you discern God's will?

What spiritual discipline(s) would you like to incorporate more into your life? It has been suggested that it takes at least three weeks to form a new habit. In the next three weeks, what could you do to cement a new spiritual discipline into your schedule?

Heartfelt Confession

Saul's creative obedience may be obvious to us as disobedience, but it is harder to spot our own tendencies toward mission drift. As we grow spiritually, we become more sensitive to the Holy Spirit's conviction, moving us away from justifying sin and toward confessing it. Over time we may recognize that sharing a prayer concern is really gossip, that aggressive driving is actually reckless disregard for the safety of others, that innocent flirting is not that innocent, that returning a new outfit after wearing it for a special occasion is not honest, and that "complimentary" hotel towels are really not free.

Creative obedience grieves the heart of God and hardens our own hearts toward his work in our lives. Reflect for a moment on your own attempts at creative obedience. How is the Holy Spirit moving you away from excusing sin and toward a heartfelt confession of it? How can you keep a clearer focus on consistent obedience going forward?

Closing Prayer

Lord, forgive us for drifting away from you, for not loving justice and mercy in our daily relationships. And forgive us for failing to walk humbly with you by creatively justifying our own disobedience. Holy Spirit, convict and soften our hearts so that we seek your will and your ways much more than attempting to justify our own will and our own ways. It is our desire to do all that you ask. In Jesus' name we pray, Amen.■

The Perfect Place

Matthew 6:5–15

Main Point

As we pray for God's kingdom to come and his will to be done, we begin to loosen our grip on our own ideas of how the world should be and we become more open to God's plan.

Background

Often we think the goal of prayer is to get God to give us what we need in order to fulfill our dreams and desires. Jesus taught a different way of praying in Matthew 6. The heart of the Lord's Prayer is not asking God to address our concerns. Rather, the Lord's Prayer orients us to God's concerns for the world. God wants his name to be exalted and the ways of heaven to be demonstrated on earth. If we step back and think about it further, that's not just the point of the Lord's prayer—it's the focus of the entire Bible.

Imagine

In 1971, John Lennon released the hit song "Imagine." In that song, he describes his vision of the world as a perfect place—with no countries, no religion, nothing for people to kill or die for, everyone living in peace. This song is about Utopia, an imaginary place where everything is the way it's supposed to be, where there are no wars, no hatred, no poverty, no suffering. All you have to do is imagine it, and it can happen, the song says. Utopia is within our reach, it can be obtained by our human efforts.

It's not hard to imagine the perfect place. The problem comes when my own imperfect idea of a perfect place is different from *your* imperfect idea of a perfect place.

Is the premise of Lennon's song "Imagine" attractive to you? Why or why not? You might look up the rest of the lyrics or listen to the actual song if you can.

Where might you disagree with Lennon's vision of a perfect place? Why?

I. **Read** Matthew 6:5–8.

Take a moment to look at the setting in which Jesus presented the Lord's Prayer. What was Jesus talking about in verses 5–8? How would this have paved the way for Jesus to present the Lord's Prayer?

Was Jesus forbidding all public prayer here? Was he prohibiting the repetition of any prayer requests after we have first asked them of God? Explain.

II. **Read** Matthew 6:9–13.

To whom did Jesus direct this prayer? How is God presented here? What is the first request asking of God? For something to be hallowed means that it is holy, that it is treated with honor and respect. What does it really mean for God's name to be "hallowed"?

Heaven is a significant word in the Bible, but it can be hard for us to understand because our own ideas about that word get in the way. We tend to think of heaven as a dreamy place that is far above the earth, a place where everything is exactly like this world, only perfect. We owe this idea in large part to the ancient Greek philosopher Plato. He taught that everything on earth is an imperfect copy of a perfect original that exists in a higher realm. The Bible gives us a different picture of the relationship between heaven and earth. According to Genesis 3:8, where was God at the beginning? Where were the man and the woman? What is unique about this picture of God and people living together?

According to Revelation 21:1–3, where will God be at the end? Where will his people be? How does this picture of God and people living together compare to Genesis?

The Book of Genesis shows God creating a world where heaven and earth overlap, where God and people live together in perfect harmony. When sin entered the world, this harmony was broken; God and human beings became distanced from each another. According to Genesis 11:4, how did the human race attempt to overcome the gap between itself and God? Why do such attempts ultimately fail? With this biblical understanding of heaven in mind, how is the request in Matthew 6:10 the very opposite of what sinful people tried to do in Genesis 11:1–4?

How did Jesus fulfill the first two petitions of the Lord's Prayer?

According to this prayer, how important is our forgiveness of others? Why?

III. Read Matthew 6:14–15.

What was Jesus' focus immediately after sharing the Lord's Prayer? How might unforgiveness contribute to the broken condition of our world?

When we pray "Your kingdom come, your will be done, on earth as it is in heaven," what are we really asking? How did Jesus show us the answer in his life? his death? his resurrection?

Improving the World

If God is going to show up as he really is, and not as we want him to be, some things will need to change in our world. His perfect rule and authority will need to show up. What's ironic about the request "Your kingdom come" is that it is the opposite of what we as sinful human beings want in our world. The Bible tells us that God already gave us a perfect place in which to live. It was called Eden, which means "delight." The garden of Eden was a garden of delight, a place of peace, harmony, goodness, and plenty. There was no sickness, no death, no pain, no war. It was heaven on earth. Actually, it was heaven and earth together! We see God dwelling with people, walking, talking, and working with Adam and Eve, the first human beings. The strange thing is, Adam and Eve thought they could improve on this perfect place.

What are some ways that we are trying to improve the world today?

How do our efforts to improve life on this planet help? How do even our best efforts to improve the world create more problems?

A Broken World

When Adam and Eve were ejected from Eden, they soon discovered that imperfect people can't create a perfect place. We've been trying to create Utopia ever since then, but every time we think we've improved on things, more problems crop up. In spite of our best efforts, we see more wars, more diseases, more slavery, more sin, and more evil. Without God, this world is one big mess! Our best efforts fall far short of what is needed to "get ahead of the curve."

The discovery of antibiotic medicine has helped to curb some powerful diseases. At the same time, the use of antibiotics has created even stronger sicknesses that threaten the health of many.

What do you see as the relationship between the introduction of sin into the world and the "brokenness" of immune systems, the weather, and other parts of nature?

Think of something you would like to change in our world today. If that change were to occur, what might be an unintended negative consequence?

Your Kingdom Come

In this world we need less Utopia and more of God's kingdom. The seed of God's kingdom is already here, because Jesus has come to die and rise for us and because Jesus by his Spirit is living in those who have trusted in him. When we pray "Your kingdom come, your will be done," we are not only asking for Jesus to make this world a perfect place, we are committing ourselves to be a part of his plan to bring heaven and earth together again. This week, commit to praying the Lord's Prayer as part of your daily prayer time.

Think about your own priorities and conduct. Are your actions in line with God's heavenly priorities, or are you just working to create your own little Utopia? Are you seeking your kingdom, your way in the situations you face, or are you seeking the high way of God's kingdom? Explain.

Read Matthew 6:33. What would it look like for God to rule your thoughts? your finances? your sexuality? your marriage? your work? your words?

Closing Prayer

Lord Jesus, how we thank you for providing for us and for honoring the Father's name by bringing heaven and earth together in your perfect life, death, and resurrection. Forgive us when we seek our own Utopia through selfishness, stubbornness, and unforgiveness. Help us to discover your perfect will by honoring your name, by forgiving others, and by seeking first the priorities of your kingdom, on earth as it is in heaven. In Jesus' name we pray, Amen. ∎

L4

A Journey of Next Steps

Luke 5:1–11

Main Point

Discerning God's will involves faith, and faith in Jesus Christ is a journey of next steps, steps in which Jesus invites us increasingly to trust him and give him control.

Background

Early in Jesus' earthly ministry, he invited a group of men on a journey. Like other Jewish rabbis of that time, Jesus carefully selected the students he wanted to go with him. But unlike the other rabbis, Jesus did not choose the most educated or influential members of society. His followers were blue-collar workers, outcasts, and political extremists. Jesus' goal was not to catapult himself to fame by picking the cream of the crop. Instead, his plan was to develop ordinary people in an extraordinary way in order to accomplish his Father's will. How would he do this? One step at a time.

Learning a foreign language, following a complicated recipe, and repairing a car all involve multiple, time-consuming steps. How do you tend to react to tasks that take more than a few steps? Why? Describe a pertinent situation.

Believing in God is just one step, but underneath the surface there are multiple steps that faith requires us to take. What makes you impatient in your relationship with God? What things do you wish were easier for you?

I. Read Luke 5:1–4.

Where was Jesus? Who was with Jesus and what were they doing? What did Jesus see? Who did he see and what were they doing?

What do you think Simon and the others thought when Jesus just jumped into Simon's boat? Why? What do you think Jesus taught the people from the boat?

What did Jesus ask Simon to do? What was Jesus' purpose—to help Simon in his work, do some sort of miracle, incorporate an object lesson into his teaching, or something else? Explain.

II. Read Luke 5:5–7.

What sort of tone do you think Simon used in replying to Jesus' request? Was he simply agreeing to do what Jesus asked? Was there a tinge of sarcasm or disbelief that Jesus was asking him to do the same thing he had been doing all night with no success? Why do you say so?

What was the result of Simon's obedience? What do you think was going through the minds of his partners as they witnessed this miraculous haul of fish?

III. Read Luke 5:8–11.

How did Simon react to the record haul of fish? Put yourself in Simon's shoes. What might cause you to react as he did? How does an awareness of the power and presence of God leave us in awe and wonder?

How did Jesus' response in verse 10 change the whole conversation? How did Simon and his fishing partners react to Jesus' second invitation? What caused them to leave behind their livelihood and their families—everything they knew and depended on?

In this story we see a definite progression in Jesus' relationship with Simon, also known as Peter. Jesus called him to take steps that increased in their degree of difficulty and risk. When Peter moved into water over his head, he faced a dilemma: *Do I rely on myself and my own resources, or can I trust Jesus?* Faith always involves risk, but Jesus does not call us to blind faith. He provides us with sufficient light to mark our path. What evidence did Jesus give Peter that he could be trusted?

Faith is trusting that while the next step may seem hard or full of danger, what Jesus has in mind is not to harm us but to do us good. Jesus went down to the depths on the cross and rose again so that we might stay afloat as we follow him. With Jesus there's always a next step, a new truth to discover, new freedom from sin to gain, new habits to learn, new blessings to receive, a new purpose to fulfill. There's always more, because Jesus is always more! What evidence has Jesus given *you* that he can be trusted?

Moving Forward

The process of taking next steps with Jesus is called discipleship. The word *disciple* in the original language of the New Testament means a learner. A disciple is one who is learning from Jesus and following him. Jesus is not just our teacher; he is our Savior and our Lord. Sometimes we move forward in our walk with Jesus, and sometimes we experience setbacks. While our journey may be full of so-called fits and starts, one thing remains the same: our Guide is perfect, and he will be faithful to sustain us in both the highs and the lows.

In Matthew 14:22–33, what evidence do you see that Peter's faith in Jesus had grown? What were the signs that Peter still had room to grow?

Read John 21:1–7. When did this story occur in Peter's journey with Jesus? How does it remind you of Peter's encounter with Jesus in Luke 5:1–11? How was Peter's reaction here different? What had he learned along the way?

The Time Is Now

We often equate discerning God's will with having to answer big questions about our future. Young adults feel tremendous pressure to figure out their course in life. *Whom should I marry? What college major should I choose?* Older adults also wrestle with their future. *How do I know it's time for a career change? When should I retire? Should I move closer to my children or be near my aging parents?*

God's will is not something we can do tomorrow. We can only do God's will in the present, here and now, because that is where we are. As we live according to God's priorities in this moment, he builds a road that leads into his future. Jesus said that the greatest commandment is to love God with all your heart, soul, mind, and strength, and the second greatest commandment is to love your neighbor as yourself.

How can you love God and your neighbor in this very moment? How might loving God and neighbor be connected to discerning God's will?

What steps can you take right now to do God's will in the present tense?

Plotting the Route

Have you ever tried to put together a jigsaw puzzle without the benefit of a picture on the box? Discerning God's will can sometimes seem like that. We can become anxious trying to fit all the pieces of our lives together without knowing the final picture. What matters more than figuring out our destination is how we get there. In Exodus 20:1–17, God gave the people of Israel his instructions for making their way through the desert and beyond. We know these instructions as the Ten Commandments. In Matthew 22:34–40, Jesus summarized God's commandments in just two statements: love God and love your neighbor. How we travel with God and our neighbor is more important than where we end up!

What are some habits of loving God and neighbor that you want to strengthen in order to travel well as a disciple of Jesus?

What is the next step of the Jesus journey that you need to take in order to go deeper with the Lord?

Closing Prayer

Lord Jesus, we confess that we are nervous about going into deeper waters with you. At the same time we understand that it is the best place for us to be, because this is where we must rely on you. Help us to focus more on doing your will right now than on figuring out your will for tomorrow. Thank you that you are with us every step of the way. In your name we pray, Amen. ■

L5

A Different Purpose

Romans 12:1–8

Main Point

As we serve God, we pour out the new life that Jesus has poured into us, and in doing so we discover a different purpose, also known as God's will.

Background

In Romans 11, the apostle Paul wrapped up a section in which he was wrestling with the mysteries of God's will concerning the people of Israel. Paul concluded that God's ways were beyond his ability to comprehend. He recognized God as the Creator and goal of all things who is worthy of all praise (Rom 11:36). In chapter 12, Paul turned his attention to the matter of how we should live in light of what God has done. The answer is not simply to take God's blessings and run, but to discover our identity as part of a new community of people who are working toward God's perfect purposes.

Opening the Can

Two hundred years ago, the French emperor Napoleon was looking for a way to get food to his front-line soldiers before it spoiled. To solve the problem, Napoleon held a contest and offered a prize for the best solution. The man who won invented the sealed can. While this metal container did a splendid job of preserving food, another problem soon surfaced—there was no easy way to open it! Soldiers were forced to use hammers, rocks, and knives in an attempt to get to their meals. It would be another fifty years before someone invented a crude can opener. At first these openers were only available at food stores. People would have to buy a can and open it on the spot, or come back to the store with the can whenever they wanted to use it. This was not very effective.

As Christians, we are called to bring the life-giving message of Jesus to the front lines of our world. Sadly, many believers mistakenly think that the only place they can serve God is in a church setting. What is *your* view? How is such a mentality like the story of the can opener?

I. **Read** Romans 12:1–2.

In verse 1, what did Paul ask the Roman Christians to do? You might compare different translations of this verse in order to understand better what Paul was saying. How can we live out these words in practical ways?

According to verse 2, how are we to offer true worship and service to God? Again, what are practical ways we can do this?

The phrase "conform to the pattern" in verse 2 suggests the expressing of an outward shape or form. The word *transformed* is from the same root as the English word *metamorphosis*, which is often associated with the changes that occur to a caterpillar or a tadpole. With this in mind, how would you describe the result of not being conformed to the world's pattern but rather being transformed by the renewing of the mind?

II. Read Romans 12:3–5.

What is the thought pattern in verse 3 that Paul urged us to change?

How does the use of the word *body* in verses 4 and 5 compare to the use of the same word in verse 1?

In light of the fact that Jesus Christ has offered his body on the cross for sinners, why is our reasonable response to offer our bodies to Jesus in humble worship and service? How does the body of Christ—other believers, the church—give context to our efforts to show the reality of Jesus to the world?

Where does 1 Corinthians 12:4 say the different gifts come from? According to the verses in Romans, how are the different gifts of God distributed? What is the ultimate purpose of the gifts (see 1 Cor 12:7 for a hint)?

After looking at Ephesians 2:8–9, what would you say is the connection between God's grace and God's gifts?

How many gifts are listed in Romans 12:6–8? Which of these gifts do you think God may have given to you? Why?

As we respond to the amazing gift of Jesus Christ through the offering of ourselves to God, as we change from a worldly view to a Christlike attitude, we increasingly discover God's "good, pleasing and perfect will" (Rom 12:2). God gives us faith to see ourselves as part of the body of Christ. We begin to recognize that we have gifts to share in order to benefit others. All that remains is for us to put those gifts to work, to use them. Thinking back to the first story you looked at, how is using our spiritual gifts in grateful service like a can opener?

Fanning the Flame

In service, we pour out the new life that Jesus has poured into us, and in doing so we discover his will and his purpose for us, a purpose that is different from anything we might have sought on our own. In 2 Timothy 1:6, Paul said the following to his young apprentice Timothy: "I remind you to fan into flame the gift of God, which is in you through the laying on of my hands." The phrase "fan into flame" literally means to revive the embers. The idea is that Timothy had received the spark of the Holy Spirit's presence and authority to enable him to share the message of Christ. In order to fulfill his purpose, he needed to develop and use what the Spirit had given him so freely.

What Spirit-given abilities would you like to develop more? Who can help you to fan your gifts into flame? Where do you see yourself using your gifts to serve the Lord?

Finding Your Passions

Our gifts and abilities are only part of our service profile. Another key component is a God-given passion. One person with a gift of teaching may have a passion for working with children, while another person may desire to use the gift of teaching with older adults. Some have a great burden to share Christ in a local church ministry, while others want to spread the message of Jesus in a business or school environment. In Romans 15:20 Paul wrote, "It has always been my ambition to preach the gospel where Christ was not known, so that I would not be building on someone else's foundation." As a missionary, Paul was passionate about bringing God's good news to places where it had never been heard, especially to Gentiles or non-Jews.

What passions do you sense God has planted in your heart? Whom do you have a burden to touch with your gifts?

How do others receive your service? What do they affirm in you?

While there are other lists of gifts in the Bible, those named in Romans 12:6–8 are a good place to start. As you look at these verses again, how might the grace of God come through your life in the use of each gift?

Closing Prayer

Heavenly Father, because of your profound mercy and amazing grace shown to us in Jesus, we offer ourselves to you in humble service. Help us to recognize what you have poured into us by your Spirit, so that we can be ready at all times to pour ourselves out in worship. Enable us to fan into flame, to develop and hone, the gifts you give us, so that Christ's love may be fully seen in our world. Amen. ∎

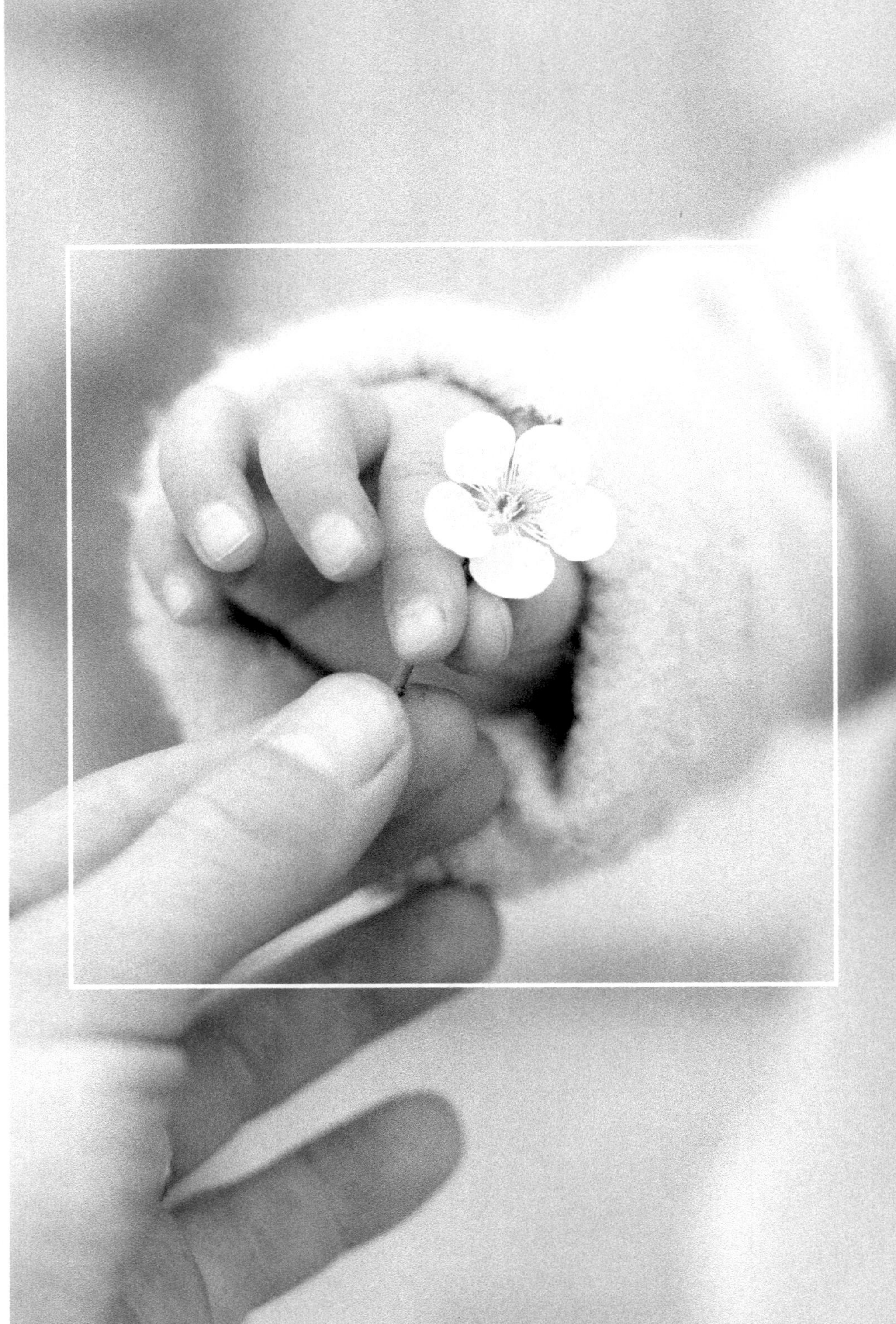

An Atmosphere of Giving

2 Corinthians 9

Main Point

When we are saturated with the undeserved gift of Jesus, we can't help but be caught up in an atmosphere of giving in order to help others get caught up in Jesus, too.

Background

In 2 Corinthians 9, the apostle Paul was writing to a group of Christians who had experienced an overwhelming shower of God's forgiveness through the gift of Jesus Christ. The message of the gospel flowed all the way from Jerusalem to Corinth, and the rushing river of Jesus flooded their lives. But for over a year, the Corinthian Christians had been hanging on to something, an offering of money that they had promised to give to the Jerusalem church. The Christians in Jerusalem were going through hard times, and in response Paul challenged the churches in his network to respond with a generous gift to help.

The Cycle of Generosity

It's called the hydrological cycle. Water comes down from the sky in various forms and makes its way to the ground, plants, animals, people, oceans, lakes, and rivers. The idea is that at some point, what comes down must go back up. Eventually, the water received below is directed skyward, and the result is even more precipitation.

But what happens when the water doesn't immediately return? That's a problem. Scientists estimate that water in the ocean can take over three thousand years to complete the cycle. Water in a lake can take one hundred years, and snow on the ground can take six months. Water is slow to go up, but once it returns to the atmosphere, how long does it take to come back down? The answer is only nine days. What is slow to go up is very quick to come down. That's not only the lesson of the hydrological cycle. According to the Bible, that's the lesson of what we might call the generosity cycle.

How does generosity travel in a circle, eventually coming back to those who practice it? How have you seen generosity returned to you as you have been generous toward others?

I. Read 2 Corinthians 9:1–5.

According to verse 2, why did Paul feel that he didn't need to write to the Corinthians about this offering? What can we conclude about the generosity of the believers at Corinth?

So why did Paul write? What did Paul *not* want? What did he want instead? What can we learn from his method of helping to ensure the completion of the thing he wanted to happen?

II. Read 2 Corinthians 9:6–11.

What image did Paul use here to describe his view of generosity? What is the principle he emphasized?

Paul described the value of intentional and enthusiastic giving. Why is this important?

Verse 9 is a quote from Psalm 112:9 that describes the way of the righteous. How does God bless the way of the righteous? Who are the sowers? What is the seed? What is the harvest?

In what way does our righteousness last eternally when we are generous?

What is the result of generosity described in verse 11, and what does that in turn produce? How does this system of "cause and effect" work?

III. Read 2 Corinthians 9:12–15.

Take note of the direction in which the blessings described in these verses flow. What goes outward, toward other people?

What goes upward, to God?

What comes down from God?

The picture Paul provided here is of an atmosphere of generosity that comes from a continuous cycle of giving. The blessings of God rain down upon his people through Jesus; this results in gifts of service that flow out toward other people and gifts of praise and thanksgiving that flow upward to God. In turn, God continues to shower his overflowing goodness and love upon those who are caught up in this atmosphere. God's plan is that we become like rivers—always flowing, always moving, always passing along the living water of Jesus to others. When you have received the amazing grace of Jesus and then responded in gratitude with gifts of money, time, service, encouragement, or compassion, how have you seen more blessings of God come down? Describe the situation. Why is giving those blessings away key to keeping them flowing and growing?

When have you or someone you know failed to join the cycle of generosity, simply taking in Jesus without a grateful response, becoming frozen and cold or spiritually stagnant? Describe the situation.

How did Jesus begin this generosity cycle? What is the only fitting response to Jesus' generosity? Why? What does grace have to do with it?

Different Forms

One of the misconceptions about God's cycle of generosity is that it is a divinely sanctioned way for believers to get rich. If padding our pocketbooks is the motive, however, we are missing the point. Nowhere does the Bible tell us that if we give money, we will automatically get more money in return. Our gifts are like water, which can exist as a liquid, a vapor, or a solid. Water can take the form of rain, snow, mist, hail, sleet, ice, and more. When we give, God's blessings will always come back in some form. There are no guarantees, however, that when we give, something will come back in the same form. That's not the point! In the end, generosity is not about what we get; it's about *who* we get. The "who" is Jesus. Every form of grateful giving points to Jesus who has freely and fully given himself for us.

How have you seen your gifts to God and to others come back to you in a different form? What has God taught you through your experiences?

A Word of Glory

There is an old song traditionally sung in church services around the time of the weekly offering. It's called the Doxology: "Praise God from whom all blessings flow; Praise him all creatures here below; Praise him above ye heavenly host; Praise Father, Son, and Holy Ghost." The word *doxology* literally means "a word of glory" and is an expression of praise to God for his many good gifts. In Romans 11:33–36 we find a doxology that may have inspired that old song: "For from him and through him and for him are all things. To him be the glory forever! Amen" (v 36).

As you look over the words of Romans 11:36, what evidence of a cycle of generosity can you recognize?

Doxologies are like a suitcase; they are often packed with rich biblical teaching about the essence and character of God. Take a moment to meditate on Romans 11:36 as a summary of the gospel, the good news of Jesus Christ. What truths about Jesus can you unpack from this verse? What does this verse tell you about the gift of God's Son?

God's Will for You

This study has been about discerning God's will. We've learned about the importance of paying attention to what God might be doing in the present moment. We've discussed the dangers of mission drift, the tendency to confuse our human goals with God's plans. We've considered the role of prayer in opening us up to God's rule in our world. We've seen how discerning God's will is often about following Jesus one step at a time. We've talked about service as a way of pouring out what God has poured into us. Finally, we've considered how entering God's atmosphere of giving can allow us to benefit from his cycle of generosity.

As you conclude the study, read 1 Thessalonians 5:16–18. What does this passage say is God's will for us? In whom do we find God's will for our lives? How so?

How do the spiritual habits described relate to what you have learned in this study?

Closing Prayer

Heavenly Father, we can never thank you sufficiently for the extravagant gift of your Son, Jesus. He is our only comfort, our only supply, and our only need. As we follow Jesus each day, pour out upon us the gifts of your Spirit, that our lives might become a doxology—an expression of praise and thanks to you. May your blessings to us always overflow in our blessings to others. To you alone be the glory! Amen. ∎

Notes